LAUREL BOY

Lessons Learned

JON ERICSON

Cover photo:
Flags at Laurel Cemetery on Memorial Day

Laurel Boy is not a history, nor even a slice of history of Laurel. For that, credit:

Edward "Roger Tryon, *Pages of History, The Story of Laurel, Nebraska, Vol. 1. FROM THE BEGINNING THROUGH 1919*

Edward Roger Tryon, edited by Lucinda Tryon, *1900–2000 Celebrate the Century, 100 Years of History, Laurel-Concord School*

We Celebrate One Hundred Years, 1883–1993, Laurel, Nebraska; Laurel Centennial Book Committee; 1992; Bryan Smith, Representative; Walsworth Publishing Company, Marceline, Missouri, 61658

Jon Ericson: ericsonjl@icloud.com

This is for and in memory of
my sister, Joan Mallatt.

Oh, such joy, laughter, and, yes, sorrow,
would be had as she read and commented
on every page, every line, every word.
She would add richness to every page
in the book. It was not to be.
February 9, 2020 . . .

My Sister

My sister died today; she was 90 years old. I am 83. I wanted her to die first.

I know how that sounds. But hear me out. She and I loved the heck out of each other. I called her every morning—for years.

As my Big Sis, she was always wondering and worrying how I was doing. She worried and wondered enough, and she loved me enough, that my death would cause her indescribable pain. The pain I feel from losing her. I would never want her to feel what I am feeling right now.

Thank goodness she went first.

CONTENTS

THE ROAD TO LAUREL

by Nancy Pickering Thomas

Laurel:
Pop. 940

That sign, which in my mind's eye never changed in the first 16 years of my life, was as wondrous as any welcome sign I have encountered in my 80-plus years, for it not only signaled that our many-mile multi-day journey to my grandparents' house was over, but was evidence that we were, in fact and at last, home.

It wasn't actually *my* home of course. I had been born in New York City and was being raised in one of its northern suburbs; it was the town where *my mother* was born in the first decade of the 20th century: where she grew up, where she attended school, and where her family still lived. Although she fully embraced big city life when she moved east, Laurel would always be for her, first and forever, "home." She and my father are buried in the Laurel Cemetery.

My parents were married in 1935 and lived in New York, where my father had secured a job. Before the responsibilities of motherhood overtook her, my mother spent those halcyon years roaming the City: visiting historic sites, museums, shops, and art galleries. At five o'clock p.m. on weekdays, she would meet my father "under the clock at the Biltmore" Hotel for an evening that began at the Roosevelt Grill with cocktails and dancing to Guy Lombardo's orchestra. In the end, she knew the City better than most native New Yorkers.

As was customary in those years before air-conditioning made City life in July bearable, young working executives sent their wives and offspring out of the heat, off to the seashores of New Jersey or Long Island or Cape Cod or to the mountain lakes of Vermont and New Hampshire, joining them there later as their own vacation schedules permitted. My mother, however, wanted to visit her family in Nebraska. And so, every June, she packed her suitcase, and later her children and their suitcases, took one train west to Chicago, and another across endless Iowa to Sioux City, to be met by her parents, who drove her the rest of the way home to Laurel.

My father had grown up in Kansas City, but he considered himself an "adopted son" of Laurel because he adored my mother and because he came to know, appreciate, and love the people and the town that framed her childhood. Indeed, her family's values of honesty, faith, industry, and education, which combined to make my mother the person she was, became his own.

In Laurel, as in all small towns in rural America where generations are so often tied to the land, the families endure. In Laurel it was the Ebmeiers, the Urwilers, the Petersons, the Wickets, the Sandbergs, the Fahnstocks, the Haskells and so many more. Their children, who had been my mother's childhood friends, were the adults I encountered during our Laurel summers. Then as now, people in Laurel were anchored in a community where, as in the classic TV series *Cheers*, "everybody knows your name." And if they didn't know *your* name, they knew to whom you "belonged," so that I, who was "Anita Felber's girl" and Alfred Felber's granddaughter, also "belonged" in Laurel. Growing up as I had in the New York suburbs, I was unused to the intimacy that is small town life, and I was amazed and charmed by it, even as a little girl.

The Laurel of my childhood summers consisted of three dimensions. First, of course, was my grandparents' 4-bedroom "Foursquare," Sears & Roebuck house, built for $5,000 in 1912.

It sits atop a hill on Cedar Street, one block "in" from the highway. Second, was the town park—which held swings and a "push-it-yourself" merry-go-round, and the ball park—with its bleachers, its score board,

The home of the A.D. Felber family in Laurel, c. 1950.

and its field lights. And third was "downtown"—which was literally Laurel's "Main Street," one block long on either side of a single intersection. There were, no doubt other businesses in those days, but the ones I remember were the bank, the post office, the movie theatre (a ticket was 9 cents for those under 12; 44 cents for adults), Harper's Dry Goods & Grocery, and Felber Drug—the last being the most important of all.

My grandfather, A. D. Felber, who had come to Laurel from St. Helena Nebraska in 1901, was the town pharmacist, and his store—complete with marble soda fountain (think here cherry cokes, "clown" sundaes, ice cream cones), wire-backed "ice cream" chairs and tables (in the earliest days there were actually booths too, with little shaded light fixtures), and a rack of magazines and comic books—was a child's paradise. Everything about that store was magical, from the hand-powered pull rope "elevator" in the back room, which was used to haul boxes of supplies, (and in those long-ago and long-remembered summers, small children) to the suffocatingly hot "upstairs," to the heated "peanut case" located next to the soda fountain with its revolving trays of cashews, almonds, walnuts, and mixed nuts.

My older brother, Jamie, our cousin Sue-Ann, and I would walk "all by ourselves" down the long hill from Nana and Granddaddy Felber's home, over the two little bridges that crossed the drainage ditches, and on to the paved streets of downtown and "the store."

Main Street, Laurel Nebraska, circa 1940s.

While most days we children were left to entertain ourselves (think here "going under the hose" and reimagining "orange crates" as cars, circus cages, or houses, or using apples from my grandfather's "7-variety" tree as missiles), there were special events too. These included Saturday nights, when farmers and townspeople, fathers and mothers, old people and children shopped or danced, went to the movies, or just socialized together along Laurel's sidewalks, sometimes until after midnight. Then there were the Fourth of July costume parades, town baseball games, sometimes a traveling circus, and Free Day, with its carnival rides for kids of all ages. As children, we were amazed and delighted by it all: we "city kids" had never seen anything to match it.

I suppose in our earliest years the ice cream delights at Felber Drug were "free." But as we grew a little older, there were "chores" to be done as "payment" for our cokes and cones. One task was to carry the cardboard cartons piled up outside the store's back door to the town dump, which was located several blocks away down a dirt road. The fact that the "dump" was perpetually burning, and that we had to get close to the fire to throw the boxes onto this odiferous and smoldering pile and could feel the intense heat, seems to have worried no one.

But this and other life lessons were also a part of the "Laurel experience;" even if your grandfather owns the store, you owe something to the enterprise, and in families, and in life, everyone has responsibilities.

Felber Drug is long gone from the Laurel of today, but what I cherish from my "Laurel days" is the sense of community that we embraced and that embraced us, all those years ago. This is the Laurel that is at the heart of the essays that Jon Ericson has written for this small volume. In each, Jon takes the truths and values he grew into in the Laurel of his childhood and applies them to the 21st century social and political issues we encounter daily. In so doing, he offers us a practical way of thinking about ourselves in relation to these issues and suggests that "lessons" he learned in the Laurel of his youth, and mine, can show us a way forward.

Clarence & Famy Ericson wedding photo,
August 16, 1922

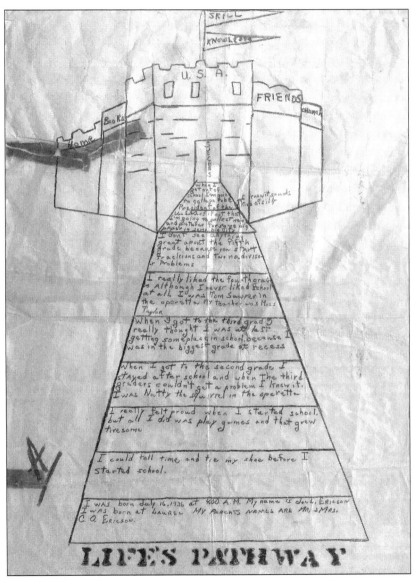

"LIFE'S PATHWAY" • Jon Ericson, 5th grade

9

LIFE'S PATHWAY *(top to bottom)*

SKILL

KNOWLEDGE

U.S.A.

Home   Books   Friends   Church

SUCCESS

When I get out of school I'm going to college to be President of the U.S. (I know it sounds kind of silly.) And if not that I'm going to collect new and pictures for some big paper in some big city.

I don't see anything great about the fifth grade because you start fractions and two no divisor problems.

I really liked the fourth grade although I never liked school at all. I was Tom Sawyer in the operetta. My teacher was Miss Taylor.

When I got to the third grade I really thought I was at last getting someplace in school because I was in the biggest grade at recess.

When I got to the second grade I stayed after school and when the third graders couldn't get a problem I knew it. I was Nutty the squirrel in the operetta.

I really felt proud when I started school, but all I did was play games and that grew tiresome.

I could tell time and tie my shoe before I started school.

I was born July 16, 1936 at 4:00 A.M. My name is Jon L. Ericson. I was born at Laurel. My parents names are Mr. & Mrs. C. O. Ericson.

A REFLECTION

Fall, 1950, as a 95-pound freshman quarterback, I entered the game against Pierce in the second quarter, and started every game for four years. "Oh my," you say, "that *must* have been a small town." At the time, nothing about Laurel looked small, but given that I could neither run, block, nor tackle, maybe you are right.

* * *

Fall, 1954, as I sat in the PX at Fort Bliss, Texas, it dawned on me that Laurel's season-opening game against Hartington was about to begin. Looking at others in the PX, it appeared no one cared. Whether shopping, drinking, eating, or resting, no one asked about The Game. Soon it dawned on me that many millions of Chinese probably didn't care either. No matter; I cared. I was a Laurel Boy. Still am.

I

MEMORIAL DAY

Color. That's what I remember most. Another word is "colorful."

Veterans, many wedged into their military uniforms, marching up main street, then boarding trucks to make the short ride to the cemetery. Yes, a short ride, but a march too far for those no longer in fighting trim. Then the flags forming a circle around the concrete centerpiece to the cemetery, each flag with the name honoring those veterans, including my father, who had marched on into the memory and appreciation of the community. As always everywhere, at the conclusion, *Taps.*

People in Laurel saw the cemetery as a crown jewel, and well-kept it was. [Even the wire fence running the east-west length in front of the cemetery was painted. I painted it. With a brush. Sprayers were not yet fashionable.]

It was called Decoration Day then, and for me, the most meaningful decoration was when I would go into the closet in my mother's bedroom, and take out my

13

father's Marine Corp uniform. I would unzip the plastic and feel the cloth—100% wool, it had to be. Made it to France and back and then remained in Laurel—in that closet that I visited nearly every time I would come home. I wonder if he wore it on Decoration Day?

Why did I never ask my mother or sister? Thanks to my niece, the uniform remains in the family. . . . .

My mother was treasurer for the Laurel Cemetery Association for what a friend said, "was a jillion years." The Memorial Day dinner was a major social gathering for the community, and I swear I can hear her say "served 500 dinners this year." 500? More than half the community?

No matter; it was a huge affair and she loved every minute of it. You won't hear Chicago doing that! What's more, she always held "Famy's Coffee" during the holidays.

"Coffee," I said? My mother baked for weeks before her annual coffees. She wanted a big assortment of "bars," cookies, and candy. She served her famous "Swedish coffee" made with egg shells, and it was always the best. She always decorated the serving table with flowers.

People came and went; most came and didn't want to leave. A special guest was KCAU-TV weatherman Tom Peterson of Sioux City. Not long after one of her Coffees, he was killed in in a head-on collision near Heron Lake, Minn., after trying to pass a snowplow. She was crushed by his death. Family lore has it one year when a local man who attended the coffee came back days or even weeks later with one of her silver teaspoons. He had put it in his pocket while eating and forgot about it. She was glad to get it back, but thought it was funny too.

No wonder she was awarded "Citizen of the Year." When she died, we held "Famy's Last Coffee," and what an event it was. A celebration of a life, indeed. Every year thereafter leading to Memorial Day, my sister Joan would remind me—and remind me—to send a donation to the Laurel Cemetery Association. One year I became confused and sent the donation to the Concord cemetery. Joan said she knew I would never remember, so she would have her daughter Ann handle it. And Ann does.

Memorial Day Address, Laurel, May 25, 1987

We awoke this morning to rain and thought, "It will be uncomfortable to go out. There will be mud on our shoes, rain on our clothes. It will be a bleak morning." And then we remind ourselves. It rained and there was mud from Omaha Beach to Berlin, from Guadalcanal to Iwo Jima, in Korea and in Viet Nam. So let it rain. Those we honor today fought and died in the rain, we can honor them in the rain.

Two thousand four hundred years ago, Pericles stood before the citizens of Athens and gave his funeral oration, the greatest memorial address in history. His speech was not in praise of those who fought nor a glorification of war, but in praise of the reason why those who were called were willing to fight. Twenty-four hundred years later, Pericles would ask of us what he asked of them, "Citizens of Laurel, why are you worth dying for?"

We would begin our answer with a tour of our community. We would show our residential areas, the yards and the homes all well-kept. We would show them our school, we would show them our many churches. In all that we show, one would also meet our friendly people. Soon it would be apparent that there are so many characteristics that make Laurel a good place in which to live. Our visitor would remind us, however, that the question is not what makes Laurel a good place to *live in* but what makes Laurel worth *dying for*.

I discovered the answer at age ten. On an October morning while I was on my paper route, my father was killed when he was struck by an automobile. Immediately I was taken into the community. Fern and Walter Tuttle took me to the Tuttle reunions. Leona and Earl Bass opened their arms to me. Sid Elliott taught me the dignity of work. Kay Curtis and Allen Shively spent countless hours with me when they could have spent that time with friends their age. Arnie Ebmeier became my friend. Neal Felber and his family opened their doors to me and made me a part of their family.

That experience gives meaning to the words of Pericles that citizens of Laurel, not unlike the citizens of Athens, are distinguished by "acquiring . . . our friends by conferring, not by receiving favors." I discovered your gift at age ten, yet I see it every day. My mother today receives what I received at age ten. Donna and Arnie Ebmeier, Gloria and Louie Tolles, so many of you in the community have reached out to help and to give. My life has been a life of receiving, a life of citizens of Laurel giving to me. Again, Pericles would say of you, so rich in generosity that those of us who benefit from that generosity realize, "the return we make will be a payment, not a free gift." I stand before you as a debtor to Laurel, aware that anything I do would be a payment, not a favor. I say of you, as Pericles said of the citizens of Athens, that in Laurel citizens "confer their benefits not from calculations of expediency, but from the trust that is born of freedom without thought of return." I accept my debt with the knowledge that I am the son of a mother and a father who were good citizens of Laurel, so I stand before you not only as a debtor to you, but with pride in the knowledge that it is payment, not gifts, that you return to my mother.

There is in Laurel, then, a gift of giving that makes Laurel worth dying for.

Those we honor today represent this gift of giving. Those who fought went to Europe to help Europeans, to Korea to help Koreans, to the tragedy of Viet Nam. As I am indebted to Laurel, so are we all in debt to them.

How do we carry that debt? In 1960 I was hitchhiking alone in southern France. A man driving a flatbed truck stopped and allowed me to get in the back of the truck with several children. As we were riding down the road the children began to point off in the distance and say "American, American." In the distance I saw a military cemetery. What the children meant is what Pericles meant: "For heroes have the whole earth for their tomb and, in lands far from their own, their unwritten memories live on in the life of men."

Last January, on a cold Saturday noon in Washington, D. C., I walked several blocks in the ice, snow and cold to the Viet Nam Veterans Memorial. I went to the directory, I looked up the name. I went over to the memorial, I reached up and touched the name, Don Grella. I went not because his name is etched in stone, but because his name is etched in my heart. His, and their, unwritten memorial lives on in the life of man. Today we speak of our heroes. Every day we remember them. Yes, for heroes have the whole earth for their tomb and in land far from their own, where the column with its epitaph declares it, there is enshrined in every breast a record unwritten with no tablet to preserve it, except that of the heart.

Citizens of Laurel, Pericles would not find you wanting.

Years ago, when I was in college, Neal Felber said to me, "My sister, Anita, gave you a great compliment. She said, 'Jon really loves Laurel.'" At the time, I wondered, "What kind of a compliment is that!" Now I know. Children of Laurel, look at me. The greatest compliment a community can receive is when the sons and daughters of that community leave the community but always call it home. I have lived in Des Moines for twenty years. Yet when I went to the Viet Nam memorial, I looked up those who served from my home. I looked up Don Grella from Laurel. Last night as I was driving here with my son, he would ask repeatedly, "How far is it to grandmother's?" I would always answer by telling him how close we were to being home. Those from Laurel who died, died for a community so special that those who leave always call it home.

II

ALUMNI BANQUET

Like the Memorial Day dinner, the Alumni Banquet was an opportunity for the community to gather. From Laurel, to Laurel-Concord, to Laurel-Concord-Coleridge School—names representing the endless effort by small towns to retain their schools—those attending found their classmates, but more, enjoyed celebrating the experiences they had.

My class of '54 should begin by honoring our poet laureate, Daryle.[1] It's all coming back to me: we are in Bob [Coach] Elm's class and ready to report on the assignment for the day: to write a letter to Santa Claus. I think it was a history class. One by one, we stand and report. The usual suspects thinking we are hilarious if not at least worth a chuckle, all bomb. Then Daryle stands, pauses for effect, and begins: "Dear Mr. Claus."

Game over. More than 65 years later, I can say I have

---

1 Fitting, *laureate* refers to a *laurel* wreath, which adorns the pages in the book, reflecting the touch of our designer.

never laughed so hard. (Don't get it? Maybe you had to be there. It was so good I included it in my remarks in 2005, below.) Recently, I mentioned to Daryle how he won the day. He immediately recited more of his letter. "Please, please," I said. "Daryle, you hit a home run—a bases-loaded home run; please don't get the idea anyone heard anything nor wants to hear anything after 'Dear Mr. Claus.'" . . . .

Neal's office in the back of the drugstore was my classroom. One day he offered this: The wife of a prominent man in the community came into the store to buy a hairbrush as a gift. Neal removed a brush from the display case, and put it before her on the counter. "How much is it?" she asked. "$2.49," Neal answered. Not quite what she wanted. Neal placed several others before her, for each: $2.49. None was satisfactory. Neal went to the back of the store, and in the storage area, he took a brush from a display just like those in front, wrote $4.95 on a tag, and affixed it to the brush. He placed the brush before her with the price tag in full view. "Just what I was looking for," she said.

A lesson learned. There were more.

Lessons Learned, Remarks at the Laurel-Concord Alumni Banquet, June 18, 2005

It is clear you are enjoying your class reunions; I used to do the same.

Never missed one during the first 35 years. No more. Couldn't take the lies. Classmates like Gary Tuttle and Neal Van Fossen would tell stories about the disgusting things they did during our school years. When I would express shock, they would insist I was present at the events described. More, they accused me of often being the instigator. Lies, lies, lies. And after this evening, it will be even worse. I don't need to hear Don Casey continually remind me that the award is not a popularity contest nor hear Roger Johnson saying "Don't look at me; I wasn't on the committee."

But all will be made okay by our class leader. The extraordinarily talented and incredibly decent Velma Bass will explain to them that the purpose of an award is *not to separate one from the many,* but to symbolize and celebrate the accomplishments of us all; not *to receive* recognition but *to give* thanks.

Because I lost my father at age 10, more than most I have been the recipient of and surrounded by the attention, caring, and support from a community called Laurel. Through the alley to Willard and Mabel Tangeman's house playing with Don's collection of trucks and riding the D & T transfer to Sioux City; up the west hill to Walt and Fern Tuttle's home to be included in the Tuttle reunion [which included a thousand Dickeys]; down to the Logan Valley Creamery where Sid Elliott taught the full meaning of the word, WORK; to Joyce's father, my uncle Clyde Shively, who warned, while so young, not to hurt my arm by trying to throw a curveball [and who did such a good job that I never did learn to throw one] . . . all surrounded me with *lessons I needed to learn.*

To Neal and Maxine Felber who not only opened their home to me but included me as a member of their family. Who taught me everything from playing bridge to playing Santa Claus. Yes, Neal had a Santa Claus outfit; would stuff pillows and me into it, and on Christmas Eve I would arrive at the front door with gifts for those in need. The gifts would always be from Santa, never from Neal. A lesson learned.

To Arnie and Donna Ebmeier who said they had room for me in their lives and who proved it by giving me time and attention beyond measure.

To the ball park where one night on the mound, I looked around and saw Allen Shively at third base, Ole Mallatt at second, Jerry Hish in centerfield, and Kay Curtis catching. Here I was, just a kid, surrounded by my mentors, my heroes, providing not only support on the field but serving as a metaphor and reminder of being surrounded by support in the community.

And what a pleasure to know that when run, block,

tackle and kick are the measures of a football player, the greatest player in the history of Nebraska football is from Laurel, Kay Curtis.

At the banquet with Kay Curtis

Sometimes of course, support comes in strange ways. One night, the first batter hit a single; then another single, then another; then a home run. 4 to nothing. This is what in baseball is called "silencing the home crowd." As I stood out there, from the silence came Arnie Ebmeier's voice, "Throw it and duck, Jon." Arnie's words were magic: We won the game, 5 to 4.

"Throw it and duck, Jon."

Lessons learned came not only in sports. Want to be in the presence of courage? Sit with Marian Mallatt. Just don't mention my name. Marian has an unfortunate habit of reacting to any mention of my name by reciting what happened when I went to her asking if she would teach me to sing. She sat me down and said before we talk about singing, she wanted it made perfectly clear that I would do exactly whatever she said. If she said the sky was purple, the sky was purple. If she said the grass is blue, the grass is blue. A rough translation is that she wasn't going to put up with my nonsense. I have absolutely no recollection of any such conversation [if it can be called a conversation since she did all of the talking], but given that she has told the story a thousand times, there is an outside chance it is true.

Maybe I could be a bit difficult. This afternoon at the cemetery, I noticed the gravestone of Mick Dalton. It reminded me of the year we were negotiating whether I would play that summer for Laurel. Everything was set if he would find me a job. Everything he found, I found unattractive. While home on spring break, we met on main street and he bellowed, "Hell Jon, if I find the kind of job you want, I'll take it myself."

On my way from Lincoln to school in Madison, Wisconsin, I arrived just after a terrible storm hit the city. Although I would be home only briefly, I went to the city office and asked Ole Mallatt for a job. Learning my lesson from Mick, I told myself I would take whatever was offered. [But with my two college degrees, surely he would find work for me in an office.] Ole took me to a room, handed me two hip boots, turned me over to Harry Huddleston who promptly took me to a manhole, removed the cover and put me down in the sewer. When I went for lunch to Lony's Café where my mother worked, they wouldn't let me in the door. They told me to go around to the back and sit on the steps, where they brought me my lunch. I have no recollection of what I did in the sewer but I shall never forget being there. And I can say I have seen a part of Laurel that most of you have never seen.

The next day, Harry took me to a tractor that had a loader on the front and a long ladder someway attached to the loader. With the loader down, the ladder stuck up only slightly and Harry told me to crawl to the top and he tied me to the ladder and handed me a saw. Up main street we went and when we came to the first tree that had suffered storm damage, he said "Are you ready? Hold on." And up I went, not slowly, but like an astronaut. When finished, Harry would say, "Are you ready? Hold on" and down I would come. Not slowly but like a shot. Up Main Street we went: Up down, up down, up down. When the week ended, I had learned a valuable lesson: Never ask Ole Mallatt for a job.

So we learn much not only *from* Laurel but *about* Laurel, but one mystery remains: While growing up, Laurel had only two Democrats: Inge Pederson and Kay Mittlestadt. Inge and Kay were considered to be a bit . . . strange, a bit weird. I was never able to sort out whether they were weird because they were Democrats or Democrats because they were weird.

As alumni, we recognize how fortunate we were to grow up in a community that understood the importance of building an excellent school. Now two communities have come together to build the Laurel-Concord school. Even though it is larger today than when I attended, I recall that first day walking with my sister and stepping up onto the road bordering the big ditch. Clutching my pencil box with both hands, there in the morning mist, I saw the school. It looked the size of the Eiffel Tower. Soon it was second grade with Effie Anderson, eighth grade with Miss Steffen, then high school with Micki & Jerry Hish, Al Papik and many others. High school was a treasure of memorable moments, none more memorable than when Bob Elm assigned us to write letters to Santa Claus. Each of us trying to be funnier than the other. Then came Daryle Urwiler's turn. Daryle began: "Dear Mr. Claus."

Several years ago, my son and I toured the school. It was summer; except for one teacher the building was empty. Taking us through every nook and cranny, giving us time he had no requirement to give, it was clear he had a love for the school and a passion for what he taught. At the end of the tour, he took us outside where all kinds of space exploration equipment was stored. He said it was worth a million dollars and with the help of Senator Bob Kerrey, he had obtained it from NASA. Sure. And I'm an astronaut. My son and I had met a passionate teacher who was also nuts. Not long after, a short article in the *Omaha World Herald* noted that Senator Bob Kerrey had appeared at Laurel-Concord school to celebrate the school's acquisition of scientific equipment from NASA in Houston.

A year later, Senator Kerrey was at a fundraiser in Des Moines. I introduced myself by saying I was from Laurel. Aren't we all. I mentioned the crazy teacher, and we were off and talking about Laurel-Concord school. Felt good. Later when I was on a far end of the deck, I heard someone call out "Jon!" I looked through the crowd and it was Senator Kerrey talking with my wife, Mary. "We're talking about Laurel," he said.

Don't we all.

For those of you in the classes of '45 and '55, most of those who surrounded you are gone. But replacements arrive, some who return to give back. David and Linda Felber could live wherever they want. They chose Laurel. Then Neal, now Dave.

Gloria Tolles returned more than twenty years ago. She didn't return alone. We have so many Doctor's degrees. We need one more: a Doctor of Giving. And the first recipient will be Louie Tolles.

One last visit to the ball diamond. We are playing Osmond. I'm pitching. Probably halfway through the game maybe with us leading 1–0, the umpire, weary of complaining by some Osmond players, calls the game and we win by forfeit. Such a commotion in the third-base dugout: Catcher's shin-guards flying out of the dugout; people screaming. So I turn to walk to the first base dugout just as the very huge first baseman for Osmond whom, surprise, I had just walked, heads for his dugout. As our paths cross, I, in a chatty mood, say, "We don't want to win this way" and if I had stopped, maybe the action would have remained in the Osmond dugout. Sadly, I decide to add that I thought the pitch I threw for ball four looked pretty good. Next thing I know I am on my knee with blood coming out of my mouth, and I am checking to see if I have all of my teeth.

In the grandstand is a couple from New York City who is driving from New York to California. Once checked into the motel, they noticed the ball-park lights on and decided to see what the attraction is. Little could they know. When it was over, they turned to Elmer and Edna Christensen and said, "We often go to games at Yankee stadium and we have never seen anything as exciting as this."

Three good things came from the evening: We won the game; I had all of my teeth, and the couple from New York had a heck of a story to tell when they got to California.

They had a story about Laurel.
Don't we all.

III

FREEDOM

One spring day—latter 1950s—while home from Lincoln for spring break, I was in the drugstore carrying an umbrella because it had been raining. Neal Felber took me aside and suggested leaving the umbrella in the store. In Laurel, real men didn't carry umbrellas. Returning to the university, I could carry my umbrella. As in Laurel, I was free to be like everyone else.

That's it? I'm free only to be like everyone else? I confronted that question when, while living in Des Moines and serving on the faculty at Drake university, the Iowa Supreme Court ruled unanimously legalizing gay marriage. Soon Evangelicals and other conservatives mounted a drive to remove three of the Judges who were up for re-election.

They succeeded. My thoughts are in the piece below. *Des Moines Register* columnist Marc Hansen wrote a column about the piece entitled: "Core of same-sex marriage issue is freedom." Freedom: we hear a lot about that word today. Is my freedom limited to being like everyone else? Is my freedom license for me to hurt those different from me? Makes me wonder, ponder . . . think. How would I feel if I were the one who is different?

Mr. Hansen,

I am a gay man who will be celebrating my committed relationship of 7 years, and legal marriage of 1 year next Thursday. I work hard for a living, I pay taxes, I volunteer, I donate to charity, I am involved in my community, I served 6 years in the military defending my country, I believe in god, I try to do good every chance I get yet so many people hate me but have never met me. I want nothing more back from society than to be treated equal and to have a nice private anniversary dinner with the love of my life. I will celebrate every year whether it is legally recognized or not, Vander Plaats and his followers cannot take that from me. I hope Mr. Ericson's and your basic statements of what this is all about make a few people to take pause for just a few seconds from what has turned into a feeding frenzy and realize that all we want is the civil rights that you have and the majority of us just want to go on with everyday life, and "do no harm to others."

Thanks again Mr. Hansen

October 21, 2010

Growing up in Republican small-town Nebraska, I was taught two things: pay your bills and do no harm to others. Maybe that is why I am a tax-and-spend Democrat and a supporter of equal rights for those whose sexual orientation is different from mine.

Maybe it is that the alternative is the party of don't-tax-but-spend and provides a home for those in the business of hurting others.

Hurting others? I am referring to the campaign—shall we say, crusade—by pastors, priests, and Mr. Vander Plaats to deny equal rights to those who are different from them.

They find comfort in avoiding the pain they cause by repeating that they are simply defending traditional marriage. In a letter to the editor in the *Sunday Register*, Phillip Kopp said the Catholic Church's support for a constitutional convention is not an exercise in discrimination; it is "merely" to return to the public definition of marriage.

Merely.

Moving to the news section, an article "SUICIDE SURGE" begins, "A spate of teen suicides linked to anti-gay harassment. . . ."

Where on earth would someone get the idea that it is okay to harass gays?

Who provides what signals that prompt those who brutally murdered Matthew Sheppard to those who made the videotape at Rutgers to the endless acts of bullying and assaults?

One wonders: How much time each day does Mr. Vander Plaats think about the pain he causes? In "The Hangman at Home" Carl Sandburg asks the question this way:

> *What does the hangman think about*
> *When he goes home at night from work?*
> *When he sits down with his wife and*
> *Children for a cup of coffee and a*
> *Plate of ham and eggs, do they ask*
> *Him if it was a good day's work*
> *And everything went well. . . ?*

No. Questions need not be answered by those on the side of the angels.

At bottom, the question is about power—the power of a majority to decide for a minority different from them, what rights they will have, the power to tell a minority "You are free to be like me." A Constitution is the protection against this abuse of power. As noted lawyer David Boies said, "If the majority can decide the rights of a minority, why do we need a Constitution? No matter to Mr. Vander Plaats. We should not be surprised to see him standing in a doorway like George Wallace vowing "Traditional marriage now; traditional marriage tomorrow, traditional marriage forever."

As father of the bride, I began my toast:

Growing up, I always wanted to be number 1, the best, at something. Alas, the world is a demanding place.

It was not to be. No number 1. Until now; until this moment. To realize that in the course of human history, the hundreds, the thousands—the millions— of fathers of the bride have stood where I stand, yet not a single one, whether King or cobbler, has ever been happier than I am at this moment. Finally, thanks to Rob and Christine, I am—at least tied for—Number 1.

Thanks to Mr. Vander Plaats and his ilk, there is to be no such happiness for the fathers and mothers of gay sons or lesbian daughters. No happiness at all for parent or child. Only pain; only hurt. They are to be denied what Vander Plaats assumes is his constitutional right. Without giving it a moment's thought.

Speaking of giving a moment's thought, pastors and priests like Cary Gordon might post as their next sermon: "The Pain We Cause." It would be the Christian thing to do.

IV

GARY

Senior year, we had our best football team in years. Only one team would prove to be a challenge: Pierce—mean, tough, and one enrollment-size above us. We were driving for what might well be the winning touchdown;

it was fourth and one, and I called a play for Billy Mal-latt, only a sophomore, but the best player on the team, to hit between tackle and guard to get that yard.

At the line of scrimmage, I saw Pierce put nearly every player and several fans exactly where Billy was to go. So I checked off to "88," a short down-and-out pass to our all-conference end, Gary Tuttle. He catches it, and I'm a hero. Except it went off his fingertips. A pass too far.

Lesson learned: if you are going to call a pass on fourth and one, you better complete it. I was no Patrick Mahomes.

Pierce was, of course, lucky. They won because of Ray Peabody's parents. Yes, they moved to Hartington before the season began, and there went Ray. Right tackle Ray. Quiet, courteous to a fault, yes; but on the football field, Ray was a player with whom you did not mess. Now he was playing for Hartington Holy Trinity. Sure, we beat them, but where was he when we played Pierce? Add to that: a story to grip your heart, consider Neal Van Fossen. Our center: tough dude. Had knee blown out in preseason. On defense he was our left side linebacker, and I can still see him pirouetting as he operated on one knee with the other knee needing an operation. Today, that knee would not see the playing field. Tough guys, Ray and Neal; Pierce was lucky. But I repeat myself. Last I checked, the score hadn't changed.

Time has a way of sorting things—even turning defeats into victories. Friendships, for example. All those best friends when we are young. Then migration, marriage, death, through the years, we lose contact with many of those childhood friendships. A joy for me is I have retained the friendship of that left end who needed longer arms.

During dinner in Lincoln, with Gary and his wife Colleen, talk someway turned to having me stop in Lincoln on my way to my October convention in Ocean City, Maryland. I would spend time with my sister Joan, and Gary, Colleen, and I would drive to Laurel, visit classmates and other friends, and more, drive to Kansas to visit classmates Larry and Velma Bass; then drop me off at a motel at the KC airport for my flight to Baltimore and my driver to Ocean City. Whew, it sounded great. We called it The Last Hurrah.

Off we go, the flight to Denver and then to Lincoln—San Diego to Denver is always on time; flights to Lincoln, or Omaha or Des Moines are always late. As was this one.

Gary and Colleen drove from Springfield [Omaha] to pick me up and take me to a motel near their home, so we could get an early start to Laurel on Monday morning. Yes, they went out of their way to make the Monday trip shorter. When we arrived at the motel, they brought in a bottle of wine, which hit the spot, and signaled a very good time ahead.

Monday was, as expected, a full day. Colleen made arrangements for Kay and Ellen Curtis to meet us in

Wayne [15 miles from Laurel]. They were waiting when we arrived, and we had an hour together, Kay was my hero when I was young. We did the milk route [Logan Valley Creamery] together, and he pretty much kept an eye on me until he left for the University of Nebraska. He still has the scrap books—now yellow—I kept of his football career as reflected in the *Omaha World Herald* sports pages. Was wonderful to see him and Ellen even though he kept saying I sure was bigger now. Guess it took me to age 81 to be big enough to play for the Huskers. Kay's memory was scary. He remembers the day my dad was killed and also so many other events and activities.

Kay, Gary, Ellen, and Jon

From Wayne, we stopped in Concord to say hello to my cousin Darlene [Shively] Cuba. She recently had a partial hip replacement, and was slowly returning to form. Darlene was help beyond measure when my mother was in her final days at the Wayne hospital. A fun person as were her parents and brothers and sisters.

Our lunch [dinner] reservation was for noon, so entering Laurel a bit early, we drove to the cemetery. We parked in front of my parents' grave; I took a few pictures, and I realized this would be my last visit.

Next was downtown to meet classmates who joined us for lunch. Daryle Urwiler, Don Tangeman, Don Casey, Gary Tuttle, Jim Thompson, and me. Karen Wiedenfeld sent greetings by phone. Tangeman brought some of his scrapbooks, and although we make fun of him for doing so, we always enjoy looking at them.

Laurel Boys

The one other person I wanted to see was Ole Mallatt. Colleen was dogged; she made some inquires, and was told "find his blue truck and you will find him." We made one last stop at his home. The blue truck was there, and so was Ole.

Ole was on his game, and we had a wonderful visit. Ninety years old, and not slowing down a bit. He offered some seriously good reflections. Such as that it was a privilege, not a burden to take care of Marian for so many years.

After visiting with Ole, we were back on the road to Omaha, again to a motel that would be on the way to Kansas City on Tuesday.

To be able to see Kay and Ellen, Darlene, classmates, and Ole was a home run, and made for an unforgettable day.

The following day we arrived at Larry and Velma Bass' home, chatted briefly, and then downtown to lunch. Like Gary, Larry and I go way back to first years in school. Velma joined us for high school and quickly became our class leader, a role and title she holds to this day. If anyone were fool enough to run against her for class president, he would get only one vote—and that if he voted for himself.

Like Tangeman, Velma has scrapbooks galore. About everything and everyone she knows. She opened one book and out came a picture of me from an article in the *Sunday Kansas City Star*. A reporter and photographer had driven to Des Moines to interview me about college athletics. I thought the picture might prompt some praise, but Gary immediately pointed out the difference in girth from then until now.

Late afternoon, it was time to get me to the Kansas City airport.

One might think those hours riding in a car would be boring. Ho, ho, not when Gary and Colleen Tuttle are driving. They even drove the car together. I mentioned I sat in back. If only I had thought to get out my phone and video the show. Bickering, criticism, lecturing, fault-finding. . . . on and on it went regardless of which pair of hands was holding the steering wheel.

When Colleen and Gary took me to the KC airport, Larry and Velma came along, and sitting in back with me, she whispered: "Are they always like this?" "Yes," I whispered. "Isn't it marvelous?" Riding in back of the car for two days gave me a front row view of a love affair.

When I returned home, I pondered the phrase "The Last Hurrah." For Larry, for Gary, for me, maybe the trip would be our last hurrah. Three old guys. Three Laurel Boys.

June 2020

Here's my question: and please give me your honest answer. Is there currently any Republican that you support? Or better yet, has there ever been a Republican you have voted for? I am just curious....

Gary

[I'm aware, you will mumble, you ask me a question that takes one word to answer, and I give you a book-length reply. That's what you get for thinking you can get a simple answer from a college professor. More, your question gives me an opportunity to put into writing why I am what I am politically. Thanks.]

Dear Gary,

Your question deserves a serious answer, and I will try to give one. Actually, two answers, along with the right to modify tomorrow what I write today.

First answer is we eat what we are fed. While we were growing up in Laurel, we were fed a steady diet of Republican. We ate it and at graduation from high school we were Republicans. We are what we eat. You remained in that culture and not surprisingly remain a Republican. I moved to a different culture and ate what it fed me. That culture was higher education. Brainwashed by those commie professors is the answer I guess. Or, while growing up, we were brainwashed [sheltered] by small-town conservatism. My smart-aleck reply is that I started reading books.

I was changing in the army and as a student at Nebraska and Wisconsin before I became a college professor. Truth be told, I voted for Nixon rather than Kennedy for President in 1960. I deposited my ballot at the United States Embassy in Rome, then that evening watched [a rerun, I think of] the first debate, and immediately wanted my ballot back. It was my last Republican vote. That may be the short answer to your question.

The second answer is that I became a Democrat because of the civil rights movement. For that, we have to begin with now, and work our way back.

"Now" means Trump, and what he reveals can set the stage for why I became a Democrat.

During the Republican campaign in 2016, I was so fearful of Ted Cruz that I said Trump would be better. Why? Trump was a buffoon and might well be as much a Democrat as a Republican. It was clear he believed in nothing except self promotion.

Then two things happened.

John McGraw happened, and Michael Diehl happened.

An elderly goon who sucker-punched a black protester at a Donald Trump rally in North Carolina said he has no regrets about his hateful actions and warned the level of violence could be ramped up.

Shortly after the incident, McGraw defended his actions: "He deserved it," McGraw said of Jones.

"The next time we see him, we might have to kill him. We don't know who he is. He might be with a terrorist organization."

John McGraw showed little remorse for the attack.

"You bet I liked it. Knocking the hell out of that big mouth," McGraw continued. "No. 1, we don't know if he's ISIS. We don't know who he is, but we know he's not acting like an American."[2]

John McGraw, who looks like you and me, sucker punched a black man because . . . he could. Or thought, because of his white privilege, he could. If possible to be more pathetic than sucker-punching a guy, John's reasons were even worse. He did this at a Trump rally. Did Trump jump down from the stage and tell John he was a coward and get the hell out? I don't think so. Anyway, that was my first realization that being flippant about Trump was a mistake. Think Laurel: what would we do if a guy sucker-punched someone? And of the person who said it is no big deal?

---

2 https://www.nydailynews.com/news/politics/man-punched-protester -trump-rally-hints-violence-article-1.2560288

Then this:

> Retired piano dealer Michael Diehl says he has
> 30,000 reasons not to vote for Donald Trump
> for president.
>
> The small businessman said he won a bid in
> 1989 to supply $100,000 worth of grand pianos
> to Trump's Taj Mahal casino in Atlantic City
> but was still waiting to be paid months after
> delivery. The gambling mecca finally told him it
> ran into financial difficulties and could only give
> him 70 cents on the dollar.
>
> Diehl, 88, told NBC News that even though
> he held up his end of the contract, he felt he had
> no choice but to take the discounted payment
> and lose $30,000—or about a third of his yearly
> income.
>
> "I needed the money because the manufac-
> turers needed to be paid," he said. "It hurt. It was
> hard to get over."[3]

So a guy, who seems cool and knows how to make
money, moves to Laurel. We welcome him, because,
well, that is what we do. Soon we hear the plumber
has a contract to fix things in this guy's house, and
the guy pays him only 80% of the bill. Stuff happens,
maybe our buddy the plumber screwed up. Then our
buddy who had a contract to build a garage attached

---

3 https://www.nbcnews.com/news/us-news/hundreds-claim-donald
-trump-doesn-t-pay-his-bills-n589261

to the guy's house told us he was paid 70% of the agreement, and was told he could sue if he didn't like it. Our buddy doesn't do shoddy work; we know it. How many of these instances would we tolerate, excuse, or joke about before we met with this cool guy and told him he should probably move on: we don't operate his way in Laurel?

Yet, lots of people in Laurel—maybe even you— voted for him.

Growing up in Laurel with whatever faults it means, taught me you don't treat people like that. Doing so is worse than a sucker punch. I couldn't vote for a person who I would throw out of Laurel. And we haven't even mentioned the endless list of disgusting things he has said about almost anyone Not White.

I know it is fashionable to say "I didn't vote for Trump; I voted against Hillary." Good try. Lying to self it is called. On the ballot, there was no box to check "Vote against Hillary." You voted for Trump. And everyone gets another shot this November. No one votes against Biden. We vote for Trump or we vote for Biden.

Why begin with Trump for my second answer to your question? Because at base, his campaign was about making it okay to hurt people different [lesser] from you. With Trump, most any day we read of him trying to reduce rights of LGBT people, and state legislatures like Iowa and Idaho are all too happy to join in the hurting. Just Trump, not the Republican party? Check the national party platform on gay marriage.

So there you have it; my introduction to why I am a Democrat: I do not believe in a party that justifies hurting those different from me. As I wrote in an op-ed on gay marriage [See page 35]:

Growing up in Republican small-town Nebraska, I was taught two things: pay your bills and do no harm to others. Maybe that is why I am a tax-and-spend Democrat and a supporter of equal rights for those whose sexual orientation is different from mine.

Maybe it is that the alternative is the party of don't-tax-but-spend and provides a home for those in the business of hurting others.

Hurting others? I am referring to the campaign—shall we say, crusade—by pastors, priests, and Mr. Vander Plaats to deny equal rights to those who are different from them.

They find comfort in avoiding the pain they cause by repeating that they are simply defending traditional marriage. In a letter to the editor in the *Sunday Register*, Phillip Kopp said the Catholic Church's support for a constitutional convention is not an exercise in discrimination; it is "merely" to return to the public definition of marriage.

Merely.

Of course, Trump didn't turn the party into a Party of Hurters, Nixon gave a major boost with his southern strategy after LBJ signed the civil rights laws and said doing so would drive the Southern Democrats out of the party and cause Democrats to lose elections for a long time. He was right, and it was my proudest moment as a Democrat.

No doubt the temptation was too strong, but we can dream: what if Nixon had said: "Many Republicans supported this historic vote to address a grievous scar in our history. As Southern Democrats threaten to leave their party, let me make it clear, you will not find a home in the party of Lincoln." Of course, he couldn't; the racist strain was in the party before Nixon.

So we would have had a rerun of the pathetic Dixiecrat Party, losers, but the two major parties could debate and decide the endless lists of issues that come before our country. With neither party playing to race.

Back to Laurel. . . .

brazil nuts were . . . n. . . toes
I'm free, white, and 21
Jew me down
"Eeny, meeny, miny, moe, catch a n. . . by the toe

These were simply phrases we learned without giving thought to what they meant. They are all the product of White Privilege. That is what we were fed.

Recently, you wrote, "we literally stole the land from the Indians, er...native Americans, and the video makes no bones about it."

Yep, growing up, we were fed bones about it, as in lied to about our history. There is no Make America Great Again because, in addition to what we learned in school, our history includes genocide. Men who looked like us slaughtered, killed, murdered, tricked, lied to and stole from the people who lived on this land before we got here. Iowa Senator Joni Ernst said our history has blemishes. Blemishes. Maybe she can't pronounce genocide[4].

Maybe begin with being Good; great can come later. Little—but important—steps: stop pounding on those who kneel for the national anthem for, . . well, having a different view about freedom in this country; stop pounding on LGBT people for, well, . . being different from us; stop pounding; *just stop pounding.*

So here we are: a rock-solid Republican and a silly-putty Democrat. Maybe we should be angry with one another. Anger toward those with whom we disagree seems to be the fashion of the day. I'm pleased you and I aren't fashionable. Just two Laurel boys who care deeply for one another, and for whom freedom means not only free to be like everyone else, but free to be different from one another.

Keep on keeping on,

-j

---

4 https://crooksandliars.com/2020/07/joni-ernst-says-confederacy-and-slavery

V

A BUILDER

Seventy-five years ago this October, the *Laurel Advocate* carried a eulogy to my father:

He Was a Builder

Before I write anything else in this newspaper I want to take this time to dedicate this poem to the late Mr. C. O. Ericson, a man who was a builder of goodwill and friendship from the time he entered this community until his departure from this earth on Friday, October 18:

Builder or Wrecker

I watched them tearing a building down,
A gang of men in a busy town.
With a ho-heave-ho and a lusty yell,
They swung a beam and a side wall fell.
I asked the foreman, "Are these men skilled?
Are they men you would hire if you wished to build?"
He gave a laugh and said, "No, indeed,
Just common labor is all I need.

I can easily wreck in a day or two,
What has taken the builders a year to do."
I thought to myself as I went my way
Which of these roles have I tried to play?
Am I a builder who works with care,
Measuring Life by Compass and Square?
Shaping my deeds by the Trestle-board plan,
Always doing the best I can?
Or am I a wrecker who walks around,
Never building—just tearing down?

This poem was rearranged by O. W. Money of Allen, with apologies to Paul H. Hicks.

Mr. Ericson was a builder of many good things during his lifetime, and many people and organizations will miss his helping hand for years to come.

I want to be like my dad: a builder.

With my dad, August 1946

EPILOGUE

Velma Bass

I am a Laurel Girl. Well, I was, some years ago. Now (in today's texting idiom) I suppose I would qualify as an LOL: Laurel Old Lady. And that's okay with me, even the Laugh Out Loud definition: it took me years to decide who I am, and not just who I thought I was supposed to be.

Jon and I graduated together from Laurel High School in 1954. We were "Staters" during our junior year summer and met at a dance in Lincoln while I was at Girls' State and he was at Boys' State. He ran for an office – I think he won. I didn't win an elective office – the Omaha girls knew how to swing those deals. I was appointed as an attorney and pled a case in front of the "Nebraska Supreme Court." I've wondered from time to time what my life might have been like had I gone to Law School.

Instead I followed "the plan" easily available to women then. I studied to teach elementary school (only two years required); Larry and I were married when he returned from the Navy (Jon was our best man), we quickly had two daughters, and I walked the "stay at home Mom" path. Sometimes I felt like a professional volunteer: church organist, choir accompanist, Sunday School teacher, Girl Scout leader, church Youth Group Counselor. There are wonderful lessons to be taught through each of these groups, and my Laurel background served me well. My parents were rock-solid honest folks; I had excellent teachers and mentors.

I carefully voted every year, probably mostly Republican because that's what I had been taught. Dad even squashed those pesky summer bugs and called them Democrats when they died. After all, Laurel was a Republican town in a Republican state.

Politics became more important to me when JFK ran for office and resistance to Catholics became evident among Protestants. I remember thinking why is THIS such a big deal? I voted for him: he seemed to be the most qualified for office and that's what I thought was important. As a matter of fact, I STILL think that's most important.

I have changed my voter registration back and forth from Republican to Democrat in the primaries so that I might help make certain that the best qualified candidate would be on the general election ballot. It takes a qualified person with a lot of experience to lead something as large and complex as a city, a county, a state, a nation...and lead it well.

My faith has had a great influence on my settling into the Democrat's party. It puzzles me how anyone can read Matthew chapter 23 and not see hypocrisy in ourselves as we recite "liberty and justice for all." I recall Gary's recent letter saying that his visit to an Indian center had awakened him to the fact that perhaps Native Americans hadn't always been treated fairly. We're never too old to learn, are we?

My background is completely German: my parents and grandparents remembered that Germanic people weren't treated well during WW I. Then I moved to Kansas where German soldiers had been held as prisoners of war. I learned that Japanese people had their businesses taken from them and had to move from the coast to concentration camps. My African-American friends say that racism is worse today than it has been in the past. We build walls to keep people out instead of building bridges to welcome them to come and share what we have.

We speak of love of country in one breath and spread fear of those different from us in the next: we talk patriotism and carry military-style weapons and I don't understand that. "If I had my life to live over..." but I don't. My prayer is that we can educate those who come behind us to accept the truths of our past—good and bad—and resolve to do better in the future.

A TOAST

I propose . . .

Frederic Henry's drink of choice in *A Farewell to Arms* is the martini. Mine too: Sapphire Bombay up with a twist, dry. For medicinal purposes only, of course.

For our farewell, let's toast Laurel with The Felber Old Fashioned. It has served me well all these years, even as I have had to make thousands for friends who demand "Make me an Old Fashioned—the Laurel one." One more Lesson Learned. The Laurel [Neal's] Old Fashioned, coming up:

Squirts of Angostura Bitters or better,
Australian Aromatic Bitters

Squirt of sugar

1 and a half ounces of Canadian Blend whiskey
(Must be a blend—a cheap blend works fine.
Neal used Sonny Brook, but it is out of service.)

Equal amount of water (or dry soda)

Maraschino cherry, plus a small spoon of the juice

1. Fill glass with ice.

2. Important to have equal amount whiskey and water— whatever amount that is.

3. Secret is to add the cherry juice.

. . . a toast to Laurel.

ACKNOWLEDGMENTS

Nancy Thomas with the Introduction and Velma Bass with the Epilogue: beautifully written. They did their part. And much, much more. Not only did they do their part, they helped me do mine. This is their book as much as it is mine.

A special thanks to Marc Hansen for reading—and editing—the manuscript. To learn more about the Iowa Supreme Court's unanimous decision and the reaction to it, see Tom Witosky and Marc Hansen, Equal Before the Law, How Iowa Led Americans to Marriage Equality, University of Iowa Press: https://www.amazon.com/dp/1609383494/ref=rdr_ext_tmb

Thanks to Nancy's recommendation, the book was designed by Gary Rosenberg. Dear Reader, you can see for yourself his talent—in his hands, design is another word for magic.

Made in the USA
Columbia, SC
24 April 2021